Easy Adult Color By Numbers Coloring Book of

Summer

ZenMaster Coloring Books

Copyright © 2018 by ZenMaster
All rights reserved. No part of this publication may be reproduced, distributed, or transmitted in any form or by any means, including photocopying, recording, or other electronic or mechanical methods, without the prior written permission of the publisher.

COLOR TEST PAGE

COLOR TEST PAGE

1. Pale Turquoise
2. Ocean Green
3. Como Green
4. Watercourse Green
5. Spring Leaves
6. Light Yellow
7. Flax
8. Shadow Brown
9. Mongoose
10. Rodeo Dust
11. Cold Rose
12. Trendy Lilac
13. Butterfly Bush
14. Dark Violet
15. Violet
16. Blue Violet
17. Scooter Blue
18. Sky Blue
19. Malibu Blue
20. Coral Red
21. Yellow Orange
22. Dark Pink
23. Pink
24. Disco Red
25. Maroon Flush
26. Charming Pink

1. Pale Turquoise
2. Ocean Green
3. Como Green
4. Watercourse Green
5. Spring Leaves
6. Light Yellow
7. Flax
8. Shadow Brown
9. Mongoose
10. Rodeo Dust
11. Cold Rose
12. Trendy Lilac
13. Butterfly Bush
14. Dark Violet
15. Violet
16. Blue Violet
17. Scooter Blue
18. Sky Blue
19. Malibu Blue
20. Coral Red
21. Yellow Orange
22. Dark Pink
23. Pink
24. Disco Red
25. Maroon Flush
26. Charming Pink

1. Pale Turquoise
2. Ocean Green
3. Como Green
4. Watercourse Green
5. Spring Leaves
6. Light Yellow
7. Flax
8. Shadow Brown
9. Mongoose
10. Rodeo Dust
11. Cold Rose
12. Trendy Lilac
13. Butterfly Bush
14. Dark Violet
15. Violet
16. Blue Violet
17. Scooter Blue
18. Sky Blue
19. Malibu Blue
20. Coral Red
21. Yellow Orange
22. Dark Pink
23. Pink
24. Disco Red
25. Maroon Flush
26. Charming Pink

1. Pale Turquoise
2. Ocean Green
3. Como Green
4. Watercourse Green
5. Spring Leaves
6. Light Yellow
7. Flax
8. Shadow Brown
9. Mongoose
10. Rodeo Dust
11. Cold Rose
12. Trendy Lilac
13. Butterfly Bush
14. Dark Violet
15. Violet
16. Blue Violet
17. Scooter Blue
18. Sky Blue
19. Malibu Blue
20. Coral Red
21. Yellow Orange
22. Dark Pink
23. Pink
24. Disco Red
25. Maroon Flush
26. Charming Pink

1. Pale Turquoise
2. Ocean Green
3. Como Green
4. Watercourse Green
5. Spring Leaves
6. Light Yellow
7. Flax
8. Shadow Brown
9. Mongoose
10. Rodeo Dust
11. Cold Rose
12. Trendy Lilac
13. Butterfly Bush
14. Dark Violet
15. Violet
16. Blue Violet
17. Scooter Blue
18. Sky Blue
19. Malibu Blue
20. Coral Red
21. Yellow Orange
22. Dark Pink
23. Pink
24. Disco Red
25. Maroon Flush
26. Charming Pink

1. Pale Turquoise
2. Ocean Green
3. Como Green
4. Watercourse Green
5. Spring Leaves
6. Light Yellow
7. Flax
8. Shadow Brown
9. Mongoose
10. Rodeo Dust
11. Cold Rose
12. Trendy Lilac
13. Butterfly Bush
14. Dark Violet
15. Violet
16. Blue Violet
17. Scooter Blue
18. Sky Blue
19. Malibu Blue
20. Coral Red
21. Yellow Orange
22. Dark Pink
23. Pink
24. Disco Red
25. Maroon Flush
26. Charming Pink

1. Pale Turquoise
2. Ocean Green
3. Como Green
4. Watercourse Green
5. Spring Leaves
6. Light Yellow
7. Flax
8. Shadow Brown
9. Mongoose
10. Rodeo Dust
11. Cold Rose
12. Trendy Lilac
13. Butterfly Bush
14. Dark Violet
15. Violet
16. Blue Violet
17. Scooter Blue
18. Sky Blue
19. Malibu Blue
20. Coral Red
21. Yellow Orange
22. Dark Pink
23. Pink
24. Disco Red
25. Maroon Flush
26. Charming Pink

1. Pale Turquoise
2. Ocean Green
3. Como Green
4. Watercourse Green
5. Spring Leaves
6. Light Yellow
7. Flax
8. Shadow Brown
9. Mongoose
10. Rodeo Dust
11. Cold Rose
12. Trendy Lilac
13. Butterfly Bush
14. Dark Violet
15. Violet
16. Blue Violet
17. Scooter Blue
18. Sky Blue
19. Malibu Blue
20. Coral Red
21. Yellow Orange
22. Dark Pink
23. Pink
24. Disco Red
25. Maroon Flush
26. Charming Pink

1. Pale Turquoise
2. Ocean Green
3. Como Green
4. Watercourse Green
5. Spring Leaves
6. Light Yellow
7. Flax
8. Shadow Brown
9. Mongoose
10. Rodeo Dust
11. Cold Rose
12. Trendy Lilac
13. Butterfly Bush
14. Dark Violet
15. Violet
16. Blue Violet
17. Scooter Blue
18. Sky Blue
19. Malibu Blue
20. Coral Red
21. Yellow Orange
22. Dark Pink
23. Pink
24. Disco Red
25. Maroon Flush
26. Charming Pink

1. Pale Turquoise
2. Ocean Green
3. Como Green
4. Watercourse Green
5. Spring Leaves
6. Light Yellow
7. Flax
8. Shadow Brown
9. Mongoose
10. Rodeo Dust
11. Cold Rose
12. Trendy Lilac
13. Butterfly Bush
14. Dark Violet
15. Violet
16. Blue Violet
17. Scooter Blue
18. Sky Blue
19. Malibu Blue
20. Coral Red
21. Yellow Orange
22. Dark Pink
23. Pink
24. Disco Red
25. Maroon Flush
26. Charming Pink

1. Pale Turquoise
2. Ocean Green
3. Como Green
4. Watercourse Green
5. Spring Leaves
6. Light Yellow
7. Flax
8. Shadow Brown
9. Mongoose
10. Rodeo Dust
11. Cold Rose
12. Trendy Lilac
13. Butterfly Bush
14. Dark Violet
15. Violet
16. Blue Violet
17. Scooter Blue
18. Sky Blue
19. Malibu Blue
20. Coral Red
21. Yellow Orange
22. Dark Pink
23. Pink
24. Disco Red
25. Maroon Flush
26. Charming Pink

1. Pale Turquoise
2. Ocean Green
3. Como Green
4. Watercourse Green
5. Spring Leaves
6. Light Yellow
7. Flax
8. Shadow Brown
9. Mongoose
10. Rodeo Dust
11. Cold Rose
12. Trendy Lilac
13. Butterfly Bush
14. Dark Violet
15. Violet
16. Blue Violet
17. Scooter Blue
18. Sky Blue
19. Malibu Blue
20. Coral Red
21. Yellow Orange
22. Dark Pink
23. Pink
24. Disco Red
25. Maroon Flush
26. Charming Pink

1. Pale Turquoise
2. Ocean Green
3. Como Green
4. Watercourse Green
5. Spring Leaves
6. Light Yellow
7. Flax
8. Shadow Brown
9. Mongoose
10. Rodeo Dust
11. Cold Rose
12. Trendy Lilac
13. Butterfly Bush
14. Dark Violet
15. Violet
16. Blue Violet
17. Scooter Blue
18. Sky Blue
19. Malibu Blue
20. Coral Red
21. Yellow Orange
22. Dark Pink
23. Pink
24. Disco Red
25. Maroon Flush
26. Charming Pink

1. Pale Turquoise
2. Ocean Green
3. Como Green
4. Watercourse Green
5. Spring Leaves
6. Light Yellow
7. Flax
8. Shadow Brown
9. Mongoose
10. Rodeo Dust
11. Cold Rose
12. Trendy Lilac
13. Butterfly Bush
14. Dark Violet
15. Violet
16. Blue Violet
17. Scooter Blue
18. Sky Blue
19. Malibu Blue
20. Coral Red
21. Yellow Orange
22. Dark Pink
23. Pink
24. Disco Red
25. Maroon Flush
26. Charming Pink

1. Pale Turquoise
2. Ocean Green
3. Como Green
4. Watercourse Green
5. Spring Leaves
6. Light Yellow
7. Flax
8. Shadow Brown
9. Mongoose
10. Rodeo Dust
11. Cold Rose
12. Trendy Lilac
13. Butterfly Bush
14. Dark Violet
15. Violet
16. Blue Violet
17. Scooter Blue
18. Sky Blue
19. Malibu Blue
20. Coral Red
21. Yellow Orange
22. Dark Pink
23. Pink
24. Disco Red
25. Maroon Flush
26. Charming Pink

1. Pale Turquoise
2. Ocean Green
3. Como Green
4. Watercourse Green
5. Spring Leaves
6. Light Yellow
7. Flax
8. Shadow Brown
9. Mongoose
10. Rodeo Dust
11. Cold Rose
12. Trendy Lilac
13. Butterfly Bush
14. Dark Violet
15. Violet
16. Blue Violet
17. Scooter Blue
18. Sky Blue
19. Malibu Blue
20. Coral Red
21. Yellow Orange
22. Dark Pink
23. Pink
24. Disco Red
25. Maroon Flush
26. Charming Pink

1. Pale Turquoise
2. Ocean Green
3. Como Green
4. Watercourse Green
5. Spring Leaves
6. Light Yellow
7. Flax
8. Shadow Brown
9. Mongoose
10. Rodeo Dust
11. Cold Rose
12. Trendy Lilac
13. Butterfly Bush
14. Dark Violet
15. Violet
16. Blue Violet
17. Scooter Blue
18. Sky Blue
19. Malibu Blue
20. Coral Red
21. Yellow Orange
22. Dark Pink
23. Pink
24. Disco Red
25. Maroon Flush
26. Charming Pink

1. Pale Turquoise
2. Ocean Green
3. Como Green
4. Watercourse Green
5. Spring Leaves
6. Light Yellow
7. Flax
8. Shadow Brown
9. Mongoose
10. Rodeo Dust
11. Cold Rose
12. Trendy Lilac
13. Butterfly Bush
14. Dark Violet
15. Violet
16. Blue Violet
17. Scooter Blue
18. Sky Blue
19. Malibu Blue
20. Coral Red
21. Yellow Orange
22. Dark Pink
23. Pink
24. Disco Red
25. Maroon Flush
26. Charming Pink

1. Pale Turquoise
2. Ocean Green
3. Como Green
4. Watercourse Green
5. Spring Leaves
6. Light Yellow
7. Flax
8. Shadow Brown
9. Mongoose
10. Rodeo Dust
11. Cold Rose
12. Trendy Lilac
13. Butterfly Bush
14. Dark Violet
15. Violet
16. Blue Violet
17. Scooter Blue
18. Sky Blue
19. Malibu Blue
20. Coral Red
21. Yellow Orange
22. Dark Pink
23. Pink
24. Disco Red
25. Maroon Flush
26. Charming Pink

1. Pale Turquoise
2. Ocean Green
3. Como Green
4. Watercourse Green
5. Spring Leaves
6. Light Yellow
7. Flax
8. Shadow Brown
9. Mongoose
10. Rodeo Dust
11. Cold Rose
12. Trendy Lilac
13. Butterfly Bush
14. Dark Violet
15. Violet
16. Blue Violet
17. Scooter Blue
18. Sky Blue
19. Malibu Blue
20. Coral Red
21. Yellow Orange
22. Dark Pink
23. Pink
24. Disco Red
25. Maroon Flush
26. Charming Pink

Thank you for supporting
ZenMaster Coloring Books!

I aim to make sure my customers have the most enjoyable and relaxing coloring experience possible and I would love to hear your feedback!

Please leave a review on Amazon and follow me on facebook for updates and free coloring pages!

https://www.facebook.com/zenmastercoloringbooks/

check out more of my books at:

amazon.com/author/zenmastercoloringbooks

Free Bonus Page!
from:

large print simple and easy
Horses
coloring book for adults
https://amzn.com/977777775

Also available in color by numbers!!
https://amzn.com/1977877176

Free Bonus Page!
from:

Large Pring Simple and Easy
Mandalas
Coloring Book For Adults

https://amzn.com/198151290X

Also available in color by numbers!!
https://amzn.com/198207616X

BONUS PAGE! From "Zen Coloring Notebook"

Made in the USA
Middletown, DE
27 September 2019